WALKS FOR ALL AGES
COUNTY DURHAM

WALKS FOR ALL AGES

COUNTY DURHAM

NORMAN & JUNE BUCKLEY

BRADWELL
BOOKS

Published by Bradwell Books
9 Orgreave Close Sheffield S13 9NP
Email: books@bradwellbooks.co.uk

1st Edition

ISBN: 9781909914407

Print: Gomer Press, Llandysul, Ceredigion SA44 4JL

Design by: Erik Siewko Creative, Derbyshire.
eriksiewko@gmail.com

Photograph Credits: © Norman & June Buckley

Maps: Contain Ordnance Survey data
© Crown copyright and database right 2015

Ordnance Survey licence number 100039353

The information in this book has been produced in good faith and is intended as a general guide. Bradwell Books and its authors have made all reasonable efforts to ensure that the details are correct at the time of publication. Bradwell Books and the author cannot accept any responsibility for any changes that have taken place subsequent to the book being published. It is the responsibility of individuals undertaking any of the walks listed in this publication to exercise due care and consideration for the health and wellbeing of each other in the party. Particular care should be taken if you are inexperienced. The walks in this book are not especially strenuous but individuals taking part should ensure they are fit and able to complete the walk before setting off.

INTRODUCTION

ALTHOUGH IT IS GENERALLY LESS WELL KNOWN AS WALKING COUNTRYSIDE THAN AREAS SUCH AS THE LAKE DISTRICT, THE YORKSHIRE DALES AND THE PEAK DISTRICT, COUNTY DURHAM IS NEVERTHELESS A GREAT AREA FOR WALKERS AND IS WELL PROVIDED WITH ROUTES APPROPRIATE FOR 'WALKS FOR ALL AGES'. THE DALES IN THE WEST OF THE COUNTY, PARTICULARLY WEARDALE AND TEESDALE, WITH ITS SUPERB WATERFALLS, ARE AT LEAST THE EQUAL OF ANY OF THE BETTER-KNOWN YORKSHIRE DALES.

Long known as a great coal-mining county, Durham has benefited from immense clearing-up activity since the decline of the industry. The coast, where beaches had been obliterated by millions of tons of colliery spoil, is a good example. There is now an official Durham Coast Path and National Nature Reserve, together with visitor facilities. A transformation indeed. Another notable feature is the use made of redundant railway lines. The county played a leading part in the dawn of the Industrial Revolution, when a network of early railways connected the mines, the steelworks and the ports. Many of these lines have now become official walking routes.

Added attractions to walking in County Durham are the small towns and villages, many of them of historic interest. Middleton-in-Teesdale, Blanchland, ('the prettiest village in the north-east'), Cotherstone, Romaldkirk, Barnard Castle, Bishop Auckland and St John's Chapel are just a few of the places which add to the interest of a gentle walk. The city of Durham is one of the great smaller cities of Britain. Steeped in history, with historic buildings and visitor attractions, it is the focal point of the 'Land of the Prince Bishops' and is a prime destination for visitors. Other well-known attractions include Raby Castle, the 'living museum of the north' at Beamish, Killhope Mining Museum, Shildon Railway Museum, the Tanfield Railway, Auckland Castle and the Bowes Museum.

Although the walks included in this book are, almost by definition, short and generally avoid numerous stiles or serious ascents, they embrace a wide range of landscapes. Most are circular but the use of former railway lines does encourage a linear format, using a bus service for the return in some cases.

Sections of designated long-distance footpaths such as the Teesdale Way, the Weardale Way and the Durham Coast Path have been incorporated into some of the walks. All the walks are carefully described, with the salient features, including refreshment, set out in a 'Basics' section for easy reference.

Features of interest are mentioned, many of them being illustrated by photographs, and maps are provided. The use of the recommended Ordnance Survey map does enhance the understanding and enjoyment of the countryside. Although some routes can be walked in stout shoes, there is no doubt that a pair of walking boots is much the best footwear for the variety of underfoot conditions which may be encountered.

BLANCHLAND

A LOVELY LITTLE RAMBLE BY THE SIDE OF THE CHARMING
RIVER DERWENT.

The highly regarded village of Blanchland is without doubt one of the most attractive in the north-east of England. Old stone buildings clustered around a 15th-century gatehouse and the Lord Crewe Arms hotel all contribute to its peaceful charm. There was formerly a monastery, of the Premonstratensian order, but no trace remains; the hotel is built on part of the site. The massive gatehouse bears testimony to the need to defend against Scottish raiders.

The charming River Derwent, on its way to feed the large Derwent Reservoir, forms the southern boundary of the village. In common with so much of the North Pennines, the moors around Blanchland were extensively mined, particularly in the 19th century. Much of the village was rebuilt to accommodate the miners.

THE BASICS

Distance: 1½ miles / 2.5km

Gradient: One short ascent at the far end, otherwise generally level

Severity: Easy

Approx time to walk: 1hr

Stiles: None

Map: OS Explorer 307 Consett & Derwent Reservoir

Path description: Mainly through woodland, so beware of tree roots

Start point: Public car park in centre of Blanchland village (GR NY 965504)

Parking: Public car park in Blanchland (DH8 9TA)

Dog friendly: On leads

Public toilets: In Blanchland

Nearest food: Inn and the Old School Cafe at Blanchland. A small general store sells ice cream

BLANCHLAND WALK

1. Turn right out of the car park, then right again at the village street to walk down past the archway and the Lord Crewe Arms Hotel.

2. Immediately before the bridge over the River Derwent turn right at a minor roadway, then left through a gap in a wall. There is a 'public footpath' signpost – 'Baybridge ¾ miles'. Cross a footbridge over a stream and pass a children's play area. The well-used path along the river bank is entirely straightforward, the only consideration being tree roots and a few projecting stones. In May the way is carpeted with bluebells. Go through a gap in the wall on the right and continue with the wall on the left, soon returning to the river bank. Go through two gates to continue. At a junction ignore the waymark, ahead; go left through another gap in the wall, then along a board walk, across a stream and a swamp.

3. Join a public road, turning left. Cross the bridge over the River Derwent and rise by the roadside for 70 yards.

4. Turn left to take a well-defined path into woodland. There is a waymark and a 'public footpath' signpost. The track is broad and easy to follow, quite high on the valley side, initially through plantations of Sitka spruce, Scots pine, Douglas fir and larch. Deciduous species include birch, rowan and alder growing naturally. Cross two small streams, the second with a pretty little waterfall. After a large patch of bilberry the path joins a public road just to the south of Blanchland.

5. Turn left to cross the bridge over the River Derwent and return through the village to the car park.

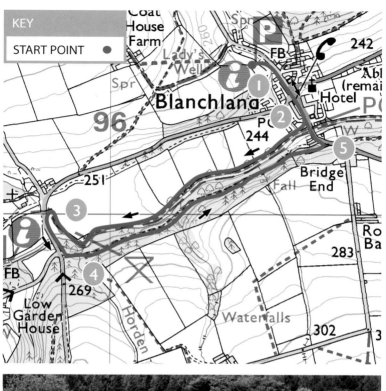

IRESHOPEBURN

A FINE SECTION OF THE WEARDALE WAY CONNECTS ST JOHN'S CHAPEL AND IRESHOPEBURN. THE RETURN ROUTE HAS THREE OPTIONS, SET OUT BELOW.

St John's Chapel is quite a substantial village with a parish church, the Golden Lion and Blue Bell inns and a little row of shops including a general store, newsagent and two cafes. The old town hall is evidence of its greater importance in the past, when St John's possessed a market charter.

At Ireshopeburn, the important feature is the combination of the Weardale Museum and High House Chapel. The latter, erected in 1760, claims to be the oldest Methodist Chapel in continuous use in the country, although that might be disputed by the chapel in Newbiggin (see Walk 7). The interior is quite striking and surprisingly spacious. The Weardale Museum packs a wealth of interest into a small space. Highlights include the Weardale Tapestry (modern) and mining exhibits. Both villages were important centres of the former mining activity in Weardale.

THE BASICS

Distance: 2¾ miles / 4.5km

Gradient: No significant ascent unless option (c) is taken (approx. 130 feet/40m)

Severity: Easy

Approx time to walk: 1½ hrs

Stiles: Four

Map: OS Explorer OL31 North Pennines

Path description: Good grassy riverside path. Across meadows in option (c)

Start point: Car park at eastern end of St John's Chapel village (GR NY 886379)

Parking: Car park as above. (DL13 1QF)

Dog friendly: On leads

Public toilets: In St John's Chapel village

Nearest food: Inns in both villages. Two cafes in St John's Chapel

IRESHOPEBURN WALK

1. Cross the road and turn left, passing the parish church. Turn right to walk down a minor roadway as far as a bridge on the left. Cross the bridge and turn right at a signposted gate. Cross a yard to a kissing gate, cross a footbridge over a stream, and cross a meadow.

2. Turn left at a junction of tracks, now on the Weardale Way. Keep a stone wall on the left, and go through a waymarked squeezer stile. Continue across more meadows and over another squeezer stile, following the obvious path, straight ahead towards farm buildings.

3. After another squeezer stile, a kissing gate and a stile, pass between the farm buildings, bearing left then right to a kissing gate. Pass a most attractive area with a weir and a footbridge. Do not cross; continue close to the river bank as far as steps rising to join a farm roadway.

4. Turn left, crossing Coronation (Queen Victoria – 1837) Bridge to join the valley road. To the left is the Weardale Museum and High House Chapel.

5. There are now three options: (a) to return by the same excellent route; (b) to go to the bus stop on the right for a short ride back to St John's – check timetables in advance as buses are infrequent; or (c) for the more adventurous a diversion up the hillside to the south of the road. The only advantage is that the height gained gives good views of a considerable length of Weardale.

6. For option (c) turn left towards the Weardale

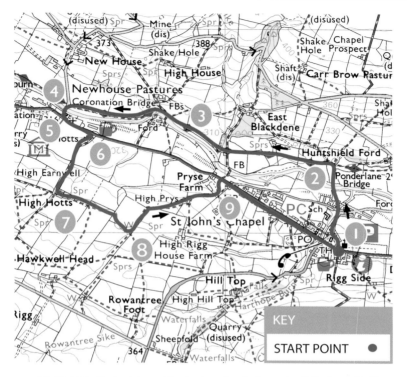

Inn. Opposite the inn take a rising track on the right, passing Hotts Farm. Continue the ascent for approximately a quarter mile to reach High Hotts Farm.

7. Turn left to walk between the farm buildings to a waymarked gate. The path is not apparent but cross two large fields heading straight from gate to gate. Cross a third field to join a stoned farm track just short of a wall at the far end, avoiding a boggy area.

8. Turn left, downhill to a stile in the corner of two walls. Go over and bear right, keeping fairly close to a fence on the right. Pass to the right of another farm, High Prys, bearing left to follow the access drive downhill to the valley road.

9. Turn right to walk along the roadside pavement back through St John's Chapel village to the car park.

STANHOPE & ASHES QUARRY

A SHORT WALK COMBINING THE DURHAM DALES CENTRE AT STANHOPE WITH THE REMAINS OF A ONCE GREAT QUARRY ON THE HILLSIDE ABOVE THE TOWN, INEVITABLY THERE IS A FAIR AMOUNT OF ASCENT BUT UNDERFOOT THE SURFACES ARE GENERALLY GOOD. THERE ARE MANY FEATURES ALONG THE WAY, PARTICULARLY FOR THOSE INTERESTED IN INDUSTRIAL HISTORY.

Well placed for access to Weardale's many attractions, such as the nearby Weardale Railway, the Weardale Museum at Ireshopeburn and the Lead Mining Museum at Killhope, Stanhope is a fine little town, with a good market place, the 12th-century parish church of St Thomas, with a Roman altar, and the modern Durham Dales Centre at its heart. The Centre includes a cafe, gift shop/information centre, units for small businesses, toilets, gardens with sculpture in local 'Frosterley Marble' and a spacious car park. One special feature, by the roadside near the parish church, is a 'fossil tree' believed to be 320 million years old.

The huge Methodist Chapel of 1871, seating no fewer than 350 people, was of great significance to the families of miners and quarrymen in the days of Stanhope's industrial importance.

On the hillside above the town was the great Ashes Quarry, for many years from the 1870s a major industrial enterprise, supplying large quantities of limestone, primarily for the ironworks at Consett. By 1920, 200 men were employed at the quarry. As the operation became progressively less economic, the quarry closed in the late 1940s.

THE BASICS

Distance: 1½ miles / 2km
Gradient: Steadily uphill on the outward part of the route
Severity: Moderate
Approx. time to walk: 1 hr
Stiles: One
Map: OS Explorer OL31 North Pennines
Path description: Stony in places but not difficult. Always clearly defined
Start point: Durham Dales Centre, Stanhope (GR NY 996393)
Parking: Large car park at Durham Dales Centre (DL13 2NB)
Dog friendly: Mostly on leads
Public toilets: Durham Dales Centre
Nearest food: Cafe at Durham Dales Centre. Inns in Stanhope

1. Leave the car park, walking through the Centre to the main road. Turn left, towards the Market Place, soon passing the amazing fossil tree.

2. Turn left into Church Lane to rise quite steeply to a 'T' junction with High Street. Turn left to pass the front of the enormous Methodist Chapel.

3. A few yards further turn right, uphill again, to follow a walled (quarrymen's?) track. Continue through a waymarked gate, now approaching great spoil heaps.

4. A gate/stile on the right and an information board marks the trackbed of a former quarry railway line and is the turning point of the return route. To see the extent of the former quarry workings continue uphill to reach two bridges across cuttings which had railway lines by means of which the limestone started its journey to Consett. To right and left are great holes in the ground which yielded limestone for so many years. Also in view are the foundations of some of the many buildings which were an essential part of the operation.

5. Turn round and return to the gate/stile at point 4. For a longer walk, after the bridges rise to a waymarked gate and follow the indicated path uphill before bending strongly to the right to walk across the hillside, well above the great excavation. The path then bends to the right to descend and rejoin the basic route. For the basic walk go over the stile at point 4 to follow the broad trackbed of the former railway line, with occasional glimpses into the great quarry hole.

6. Reach a post with two waymarks; bear right to commence the descent to Stanhope along a good path initially through woodland. On reaching a road (High Street) turn right, re-joining the outward route in a short distance. Turn left to return to the Market Square and the Durham Dales Centre.

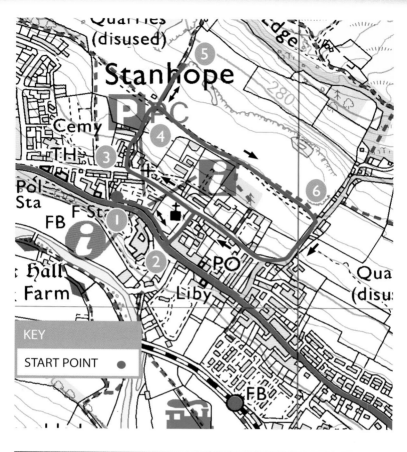

KEY

START POINT ●

FROSTERLEY

A CIRCUIT OF AN AREA OF FORMER EXTENSIVE QUARRYING, HOME OF THE 'FROSTERLEY MARBLE', A BEAUTIFUL FORM OF HARD LIMESTONE. NOT A HARD WALK BUT A FAIR AMOUNT OF RISE AND FALL.

As a village Frosterley is an unremarkable place, with a general store. However, on the opposite side of the valley of the River Wear is a huge quarrying area, now largely disused. The distinction here is the production of 'Frosterley Marble'. It is not actually a marble, but a very distinctive form of hard limestone, a sedimentary rock laid down 325 million years ago, rich in fossils and highly esteemed. The rock can be cut and polished. The disused Harehope Quarry was a great source of the stone, which can be found in the fonts of several Weardale churches, the Durham Dales Centre at Stanhope, Durham

Cathedral and much further afield. There are slabs of the stone at the car park and on the platform of Frosterley railway station.

THE BASICS

Distance: 3½ miles / 5.5km

Gradient: Two sections are steadily uphill, approximately 130 feet (40 m) in total

Severity: Generally easy

Approx time to walk: 2 hours

Stiles: Three

Map: OS Explorer OL31, North Pennines

Path description: Generally good paths & minor roads. One section of path is very narrow

Start point: Public car park in, Frosterley village (GR NZ 026370)

Parking: Public car park as above (DL13 2SF)

Dog friendly: On leads

Public toilets: None

Nearest food: Black Bull and other inns at Frosterley

FROSTERLEY WALK

1. From the car park cross the road, and turn right for 50 yards to reach a bus shelter. Turn left immediately to walk past a few garages. Follow the excellent footpath in an easterly direction, bearing left at a junction. The path separates rows of houses from parts of their gardens, with the River Wear below. There are two modern kissing gates before a road joins from the left. Cross a gated level crossing with 'Mineral Valley Walk' waymark to descend towards the river, crossed on a long footbridge.

2. Bear left along a quarry-like roadway. Go over a stile and continue, passing openings into an operational quarry (Broadwood). Walk alongside the quarry access road to a junction beside a railway crossing.

3. Go right to follow a little lane, uphill, signposted to Harehope Quarry. Pass allotments, then a gate on the right; a diversion here gives access to the eastern end of Harehope

Quarry. Continue along the road, passing modern timber buildings and rising again. Ignore a gate/stile on the right as the road bears right, uphill.

4. Turn right at a kissing gate with a Weardale Way waymark to follow a broad track along the bottom edge of a large field, towards Gill Barn. Go through a kissing gate then leave the track to the right at a second kissing gate. Continue in the same direction along a narrow path between fences, Go over a stile, bearing right to descend over grass towards another stile. To the left is a carved 'Weardale Way' seat. Pass below the seat, with a fence on the right, to a kissing gate and light woodland. There is an information board concerning a former lead mine, a stone ruin and a junction of tracks.

5. Rake back to the right along a little path which leads to an open area at the western entrance of the former Harehope Quarry where there is visitor information. Return to a bridge over Bollihope Burn. Cross, looking out for Frosterley Marble below, and immediately go left over a stile to follow a good track for some distance beside the burn. Reach a row of huge former lime kilns. Of the original set, many have collapsed and the remainder are in poor condition. Continue along the track, bearing right to

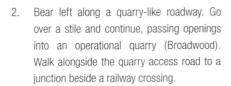

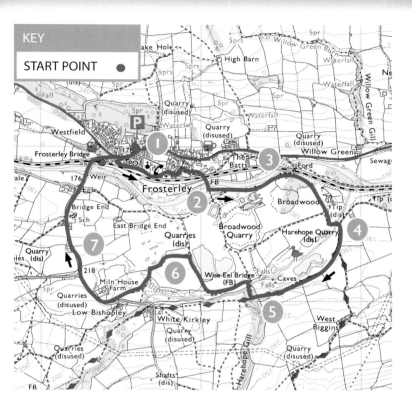

KEY

START POINT ●

two isolated former quarry or agricultural buildings.

6. The track, now a farm roadway, rises to the left towards a visible hamlet. Go through a gate to join a minor road. Turn right to walk past the entrance to Miln House Farm and reach a road junction.

7. Turn right to descend by the roadside towards the visible Frosterley village, passing a Methodist Church and the railway station and crossing the river. Pass the Black Bull Inn before bearing right at a road junction to return to the car park.

WOLSINGHAM

The Wolsingham Family Walk is a delightful, undemanding stroll involving the centre of Wolsingham together with its immediate surroundings. It is truly a walk for all ages, as most of the route is hard surfaced, enabling pushchairs and wheelchairs.

Wolsingham is a compact little town, with shops, inns and attractive old buildings clustered around a market square. The site of the former Demesne Mill, on the line of this walk, has been converted into a picnic area.

THE BASICS

Distance: 1½ miles / 2.5km

Gradient: Flat

Severity: Easy

Approx time to walk: 45 minutes

Stiles: none

Map: OS Explorer OL31, North Pennines

Path description: Hard-surfaced paths and sides of quiet roads

Start point: Recreation ground, Wolsingham (GR NZ 071372)

Parking: Public recreation ground by the side of the main road to the west of the town centre (DL13 3AS)

Dog friendly: On leads

Public toilets: Close to Market Square in Wolsingham

Nearest food: Black Bull Inn and cafes in the Market Place

WOLSINGHAM WALK

1. Walk away from the road, following a roadway along the left side of the extensive recreation area. The roadway soon becomes a surfaced path, with adjacent woodland rich in snowdrops in late winter, reaching the side of the River Wear and bearing left to continue under the iron bridge of 1884. In former times the banks of the river in this area were a hive of industry. Pass through a static caravan park to reach the south-east corner of the Market Place.

2. The Black Bull Inn is visible to the left. Bear left, crossing the road to proceed up the east side of the Market Place then along Angate Street, signposted to Tow Law. On the left the former convent has been converted attractively into modern apartments, while on the right an 18th-century three-storey house was formerly a brewery.

3. Reach the bridge over the Waskrow Beck. Do not cross; turn left to follow the track close to the beck as far as Demesne Picnic Area. This was the site of an ancient mill, demolished in 1951.

4. Continue through the picnic area, soon coming to a junction. The route goes to the left here but there is an out and back option to follow the beck a little further to view rapids and pools, known as The Sills.

5. At a junction of tracks just short of Wolsingham Community College turn left to walk towards the churchyard. Do not enter the churchyard; turn right to reach a road. Turn left to walk past a large building of the former grammar school and join the main road.

6. Turn left to return to the recreation ground and the car park.

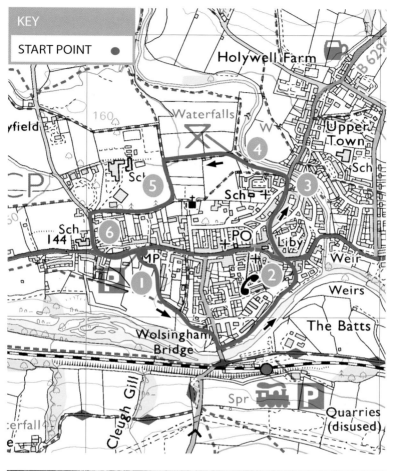

KEY

START POINT ●

Holywell Farm

Waterfalls

Upper Town

Sch

field

Sch

CP

Sch
144

PO

Lіby

Weir

Weirs

The Batts

Wolsingham Bridge

Cleugh Gill

Spr

Quarries (disused)

HIGH FORCE

A QUITE DEMANDING BUT REWARDING CIRCULAR WALK IN
THE LOVELY SCENERY OF UPPER TEESDALE, USING PART OF THE
PENNINE WAY, WITH A VIEW OF THE GREAT HIGH FORCE
WATERFALL AS A BONUS.

High Force has a good claim to be England's
finest waterfall, a great surge of the River Tees
crashing over rocks with a height of 70 feet
(21m) into a pool below. Not quite the highest
waterfall in Britain, but certainly one of the most
impressive. The river falls over the Whin Sill, an
area of very hard dolerite rock which is a volcanic
intrusion into an area of softer limestone and
sandstone. While the route set out below provides
(with care) a viewpoint for the falls, for a closer
view it is necessary to pay a modest fee at the
car park souvenir shop for the use of a privately
owned footpath.

The Pennine Way was one of the first long-distance footpaths to be created, a continuous route along the Pennine backbone of northern England, from Edale in Derbyshire to Kirk Yetholm on the Scottish border. It has provided a challenge for generations of hardy walkers.

High Force in Upper Teesdale

THE BASICS

Distance: 4¾ miles / 7.5km

Gradient: Considerable rise and fall, totalling approximately 330 feet (100m)

Severity: One of the most demanding walks in the book

Approx time to walk: 2½ hrs

Stiles: One

Map: OS Explorer OL31, North Pennines.

Path description: The Pennine Way is very varied, with some rough sections, particularly the descent to the farm, set out below. A length of roadside is used to return to the car park

Start point: High Force car park (GR NY 886286)

Parking: High Force car park (charge) (DL12 0XH)

Dog friendly: Above average

Public toilets: At car park

Nearest food: High Force Hotel

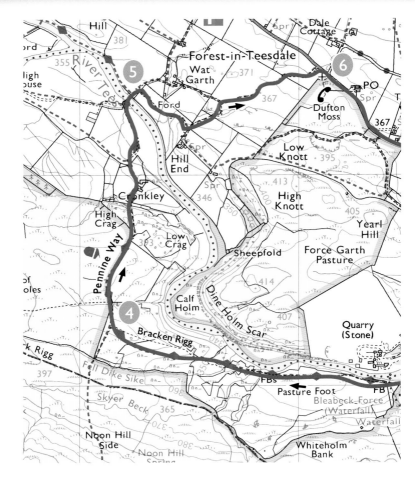

1. Leave the car park and cross the road, turning left for 40 yards. Turn right at a 'public footpath' sign to follow a path descending the wooded side of the river valley. A short flight of steps is followed by a longer flight (with handrail). After a waymarked gate bear left to continue along the broad, grassy river bank.

2. Go through a waymarked kissing gate to turn right and cross the river on a footbridge. At the far end of the bridge join the Pennine Way, turning right. This part of the Way is a good broad track, partially paved, initially climbing the river bank. Go through a kissing gate, passing a 'welcome' board to Moor House, Upper Teesdale and the National Nature Reserve. The excellent track continues, crossing a stream to a kissing gate.

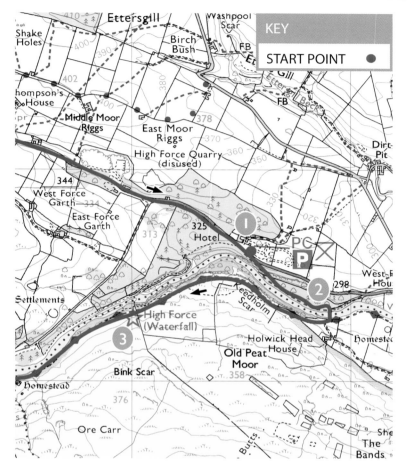

3. After a suitable warning, a right turn leads to a viewpoint for the waterfall, a diversion of 20 yards or so. Return to the main path and continue along the Way. After a kissing gate there is a rougher length of path and a large quarry on the far side of the river. Go over a waymarked stile, the path now over easy grass. There are footbridges over three tributary streams, two of them close together, then stepping stones over another stream, before starting a considerable rise, aided by sections of boardwalk and paving.

4. After passing two short marker stones the track dips to the right. Go over a stile into open access land and through a waymarked gate. Across the valley the hillside is dotted with white-painted farms (Raby Estate). Go over a gated stile on

the right to descend to the left towards a nearby farm. This descent is very rough, steep and stony. At the bottom, go through a small gate, then a wide gate on the left to rise towards the farm. Follow the signs to go round a large building, then through another gate to join the farm access roadway. Follow this roadway to reach a bridge across the river.

5. Cross the bridge and stay with a farm roadway as it rises to the right. Go over a waymarked cattle grid. On approaching Hill End Farm, keep left, soon rising gently through sheep-farming country, with prominent moorland bird activity in spring.

6. Join the Teesdale public highway; turn right to walk by the side of this generally quiet road. Pass the junction with a quarry access road. From this point there is roadside pavement all the way to the High Force Hotel and the car park.

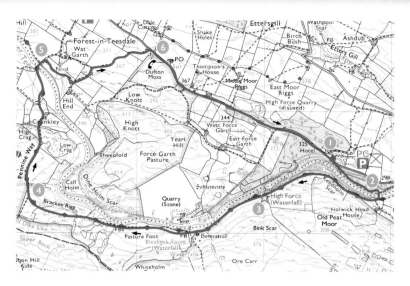

BOWLEES & LOW FORCE

This Tees Valley circular walk is based on the popular visitor centre at Bowlees, crossing the River Tees to use a short length of the Pennine Way, almost as far as Low Force waterfall. Wynch Bridge is then used to re-cross the river for the return to the visitor centre.

Bowlees Visitor Centre is housed in a former Methodist Chapel, with catering facilities, public conveniences, generous car parking and visitor information. The surrounding area is very attractive, including the wooded valley of Bow Lee Beck with paths to waterfalls and to Gibson Cave, many years ago the hideout of a wanted fugitive. The area is a nature reserve.

Newbiggin Chapel

Indenture Date Aug 1759
Cost of land £5:0,:0ᵈ
Cost of Building £61:13,:5
Pulpit used by John Wesle

Low Force is a powerful waterfall on the River Tees, where the river surges over the hard rock of the Whin Sill. Wynch Bridge is a fine suspension bridge spanning a rocky gorge through which the Tees surges with great force. It was constructed in 1830 to replace an earlier and less secure bridge which collapsed in 1803 whilst a gang of miners was passing over. One man was drowned.

Newbiggin, a recommended diversion from the course of the walk, is a village with white-painted buildings nicely clustered. Of particular interest is the Methodist Chapel of 1759, now claimed to be the oldest in the country still in regular use for worship.

THE BASICS

Distance: 2½ miles / 4km

Gradient: Almost flat with short ascents only

Severity: Gentle; one short, sharp rise after Wynch Bridge

Approx time to walk: 1½ hrs

Stiles: Three

Map: OS Explorer OL31, North Pennines

Path description: Some cattle-churned ground close to the start, otherwise good paths and a short length of the road

Start point: Main car park close to Bowlees Visitor Centre (GR NY 908281)

Parking: Large woodland car park near to visitor centre (DL12 0XE)

Dog friendly: On leads

Public Toilets: At visitor centre

Nearest food: Cafe at visitor centre

BOWLEES & LOW FORCE WALK

1. Leave the car park along a broad rising track, with public conveniences below to the left. In a little more than 50m turn left at a gate with a 'public footpath' signpost. A track rising across a meadow soon becomes obvious. As it steepens and bends strongly to the left, leave the track to head to the right towards a gate/stile. A faint path becomes apparent. After the gate continue on the same line, with a wall close on the right. The path is very vague and the ground may well be cattle-churned. Approaching the cottages at Hood Gill, keep left to a waymarked stile. Go over, keeping to the left of the cottages, to walk to a gate on the right, giving access to the approach roadway. Join the roadway, going left to walk to the main road. Continue by the roadside for approximately a quarter-mile (0.5km), passing the Newbiggin boundary sign and looking out for the start of a footpath on the right. The village is seen to the left, across a field. To visit Newbiggin (recommended) go a little further along the road, to a little road on the left, leading into the village.

2. At a 'public footpath' signpost turn right, over a stile, to enter the Raby Estate. Cross a large meadow, towards the end of a wooded knoll. Go over another stile and cross a footbridge over Bow Lee Beck. Pass the end of the wooded knoll and cross two smaller meadows to reach a long and high footbridge over the River Tees. Cross the bridge, rising to join the Pennine Way footpath.

3. Turn right to follow the Way, closely beside a delightful length of the river, with noisy rapids. Enter the Moor House National Nature Reserve, where a length of the path has stone flag paving.

4. At a well-signposted major junction, there is a fine view of Low Force, ahead. Turn right to leave the Pennine Way, by crossing Wynch Bridge. There is a short, sharp rise to a gate/stile.

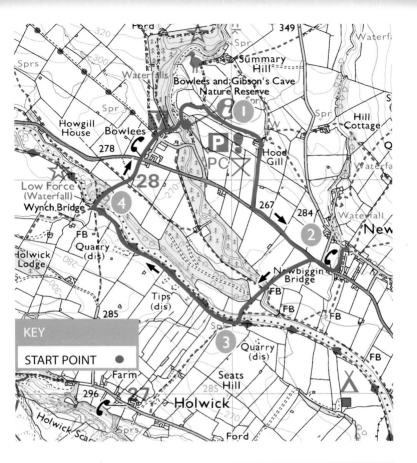

Go through and cross a small meadow to reach the main road at another gate/stile. Cross the road and take the minor roadway almost opposite to pass through Bowlees hamlet. Pass beside the visitor centre and rise a little before descending a flight of steps to a bridge over Bow Lee Beck to reach the car park.

A SECTION OF THE TEES RAILWAY PATH, PLUS A TRACK ACROSS FARMING LAND, CONNECTS THE STRAGGLING VILLAGE OF MICKLETON WITH THE LARGER MIDDLETON-IN-TEESDALE, FOCAL POINT OF THIS PART OF THE VALLEY OF THE RIVER TEES.

The walk is linear, with the return by bus needing careful scrutiny of the timetable (basically the service runs every two hours).

Middleton-in-Teesdale is an attractive large village, the unchallenged 'capital' of middle Teesdale. With inns, cafes and shops, tourist information and an hourly bus service to Barnard Castle, it is well placed for exploration of a large part of the North Pennines. A clock tower, a drinking fountain and an ancient churchyard cross are of particular interest. Historically, the London Lead Company played an important part locally, in 1823 purchasing the 'New Town' estate (the part facing the river was formerly known as 'Ten Row') as homes for miners, accessed under the ornamental Masterman Arch, which had iron gates. The miners had to be home by a certain time at night or face severe consequences. The London Lead Company ceased its local operations in 1905, after contributing a great deal to the community life of Middleton, including chapels, Sunday schools, a village band and horticultural shows.

The parish church of St Mary the Virgin of 1876 is on the site of a 12th-century church. The churchyard has the grave of Richard Watson, the 'Teesdale Poet', and an unusual detached bellhouse.

Mickleton, in contrast, is an unremarkable place, straggling along the Middleton to Romaldskirk road. It does, however, have two inns.

THE BASICS

Distance: 2½ miles / 4km

Gradient: Substantially flat

Severity: Easy, almost level walking

Approx. time: 1¼ hrs

Stiles: Three

Map: OS Explorer OL31, North Pennines

Path description: Firm trackbed of former railway line, path across meadow, farm access drive and roadside pavement

Start point: Picnic area on site of former Mickleton railway station (GR NY 968234)

Parking: Picnic area on site of the former Mickleton railway station (DL12 0JN)

Dog friendly: Yes, along former railway line; otherwise strictly on leads

Public toilets: Near bus stop in Middleton

Nearest food: Blacksmith's Arms at Mickleton; choice of cafes and inns at Middleton

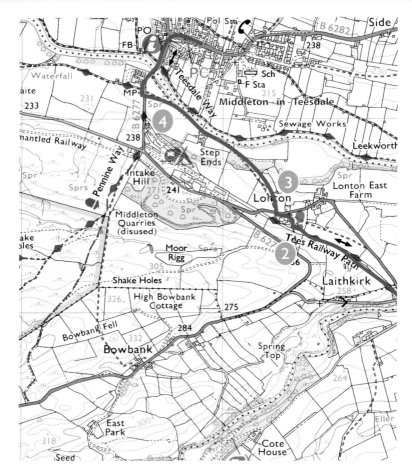

1. Leave the picnic area through a gateway at the west end. There is a 'Middleton-in-Teesdale 2 miles' sign. The former railway trackbed provides a first-class walking route, firm underfoot and predominantly level, with wide views over Teesdale. Cross over an access drive, with gates on either side. After crossing a minor lane, you come to a splendid viaduct, which carried the line over the valley of the River Lune (a tributary of the River Tees, not to be confused with its more famous namesake on the west of the Pennines).

2. Before the end of the line is reached turn right over a waymarked ladder stile, signposted to Middleton.

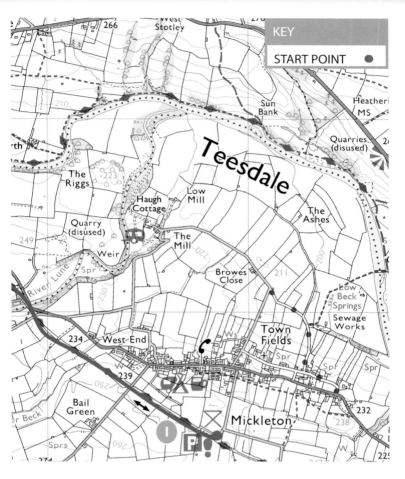

MICKLETON WALK

3. Descend a little meadow close to a farm, bearing left to a little gate and a squeezer stile in the bottom corner. Join the road, turning left for 50 yards. Go over a signposted stile to follow a path worn over grass to a stone wall with another stile. Descend a bank and continue to a gate/stile in the far corner. Follow a track past Step Ends Farm and the farm access road to a junction with the public road, almost opposite Middleton cattle market.

4. Turn right to follow the roadside pavement, then cross the bridge over the River Tees before rising into Middleton. Go right at the village centre road junction to reach the bus stop and public conveniences.

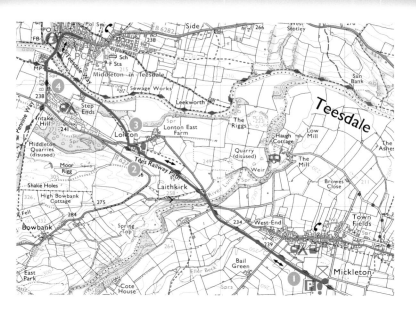

ROMALDKIRK

This linear walk, along the side of a delightful part of the valley of the River Tees, can be undertaken in either direction, using the local bus (basically a two-hourly service) for the outward or for the return journey. Alternatively, it is sufficiently short to be walked both ways.

The Tees Railway Trail forms the basis of the route, ensuring easy route-finding, a basically level format and good ground underfoot. The views across the valley are better than is usual from a railway trail.

The branch line railway connecting Middleton-in-Teesdale with Barnard Castle, Bishop Auckland and Darlington was opened in 1868, later becoming part of the extensive North Eastern Railway. It served areas in Teesdale with important mining and quarrying activities. As with so many lines in comparatively remote and sparsely populated areas it was closed after the Beeching Report, in 1964. Fortunately Durham County Council took the opportunity to create a continuous footpath and cycle way along several miles of the former trackbed. Note that a section at Romaldkirk has remained in private ownership, resulting in a detour through the village.

Romaldkirk is a delightful village, surrounding a large green, which is divided by the Kirk Inn. Across the road is the Rose and Crown, another popular hostelry, with the attractive parish church close by. The village stocks, on the green, have survived.

© Paul Buckingham

Mickleton village also has some good old buildings and two inns, but the linear shape, along both sides of the Middleton to Romaldkirk road, results in a rather straggling appearance.

The walking route is set out from Romaldkirk to Mickleton, using the bus to go back to the start at Romaldkirk. It can be done equally well in reverse, i.e. walking before riding. The bus service (96) is not very frequent; timetables are widely available locally and on the internet.

THE BASICS

Distance: 2¼ miles / 3.75km

Gradient: Flat

Severity: Easy walking

Approx time to walk: 1¼ hrs

Stiles: None

Map: OS Explorer OL31, North Pennines

Path description: Firm trackbed of former railway line & a short length of minor lane

Start Point: Rose and Crown Inn, Romaldkirk (GR NY 996221)

Parking; Roadside by the green in Romaldkirk, DL12 9EE, or (if using the bus for the outward journey) the former Mickleton railway station, DL12 0JN (see Walk 8)

Dog friendly: Yes, on leads in the villages

Public toilets: None

Nearest food: Two inns in each of the villages

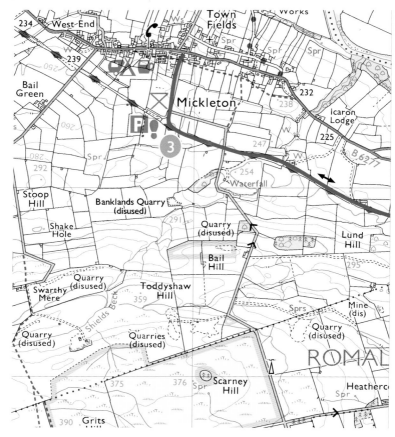

1. From the bus stop opposite the Rose and Crown, go ahead to a road junction. There are several little brown signs for the Tees Railway Walk, pointing in different directions. Go straight across to continue in the same direction along a more minor road, rising gently. After less than a quarter-mile (0.5km), on the right is the end of the former Romaldkirk railway station building, with a splendid traditional railway signal beside.

© Phillip Barker

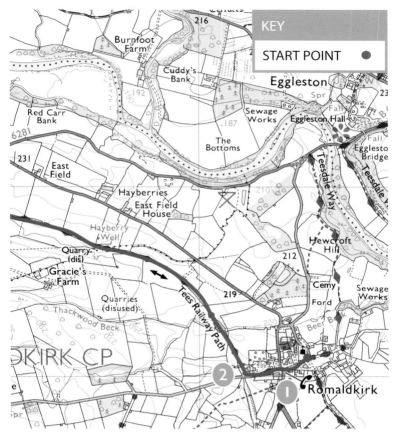

2. Stay with the road for a few yards further before turning right to rise up a sloping path, before descending on or beside a long flight of steps leading to the former trackbed. Turn left to walk for 1¾ miles (3km) toards Mickleton. The trackbed may have some mud, but the surface is generally good and the views are long and wide as the track is largely across open hillside. Eggleston village is prominent across the valley. In several places the original alignment has been marginally changed and there are several gates but no route-finding is necessary and there is never the slightest danger of straying from the intended route.

3. Reach the site of the former Mickleton station, with its visitor car park. Leave the railway line to turn right and follow a minor surfaced lane, with pavement, back to the village street, reached opposite the Blacksmith's Arms, beside the village hall car park and the bus stop.

GRASSHOLME RESERVOIR

AN ATTRACTIVE CIRCUIT OF A SUBSTANTIAL RESERVOIR.
PERHAPS SURPRISINGLY, THIS IS ONE OF THE MORE
DEMANDING WALKS IN THIS BOOK.

Crossing various streams which contribute to the reservoir necessitates a fair amount of rise and fall although there are no real hills. The path is generally good, but there are sections which might be muddy and some lengths are quite rough.

Grassholme Reservoir is an attractive sheet of water; apart from the dam it has a natural appearance, its adjacent hillsides crowned with farms and hamlets. It is readily accessible from Middleton-in-Teesdale. Part of a series of reservoirs constructed from 1896 to serve the growing population of the industrialised Middlesbrough area, this particular reservoir was started in 1910. Subject to specified rules and regulations, public access is encouraged.

THE BASICS

Distance: 3¾ miles / 6km
Gradient: Several short uphill sections
Severity: Quite steep but very short ascents
Approx. min. time to walk: 2 hrs
Stiles: None
Map: OS Explorer OL31, North Pennines
Path description: Very variable minor path, mostly good underfoot
Start Point: Grassholme Visitor Centre (GR NY 949225)
Parking: Substantial car park at Grassholme Visitor Centre (DL12 0PW)
Dog friendly: On leads (water authority requirement)
Public toilets: At Visitor Centre. Portaloo at picnic area.
Nearest food: At Visitor Centre

GRASSHOLME RESERVOIR WALK

1. Leave the parking area by the roadway leading to the disabled parking area. Note the Water Authority notice board with prohibition of many likely (and unlikely) activities. Continue through a small gate and follow the obvious path along the side of the water, soon coming to the first stream, Easter Beck, where paving has been laid and a bridge provided for walkers.

2. Carry on along the narrow path, close to a wall on the left for some distance. The path is generally easy to follow. There is another bridge, then steps down, a third bridge and steps up. Go through a gate to join a minor road, turning right, downhill, to follow the road over a long, narrow, bridge across the reservoir. At the far and of the bridge is a car parking/picnic area, with Portaloo toilet .Go through the car park to take a grassy track at the far side. This is the north shore path. Head back towards the reservoir dam, aided in places by boardwalks and with one major valley, Blind Beck, to cross, down a long flight of steps, across a bridge and a rise on the far side. The path becomes more straightforward as the dam is approached.

3. Turn right to cross the dam. At the far end turn right again to follow a paved footpath leading to the foot of a flight of steps. Turn left, up the steps, for a direct return to the car park.

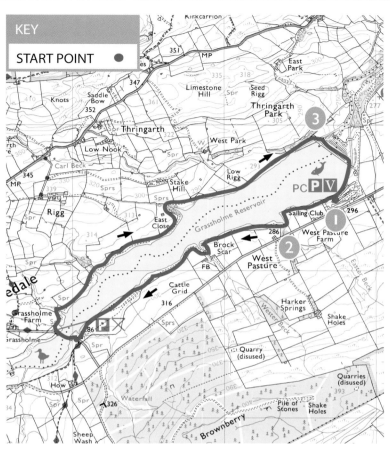

KEY

START POINT ●

BLACKTON RESERVOIR

A TRIBUTARY OF TEESDALE, BALDERSDALE IS A SUBSTANTIAL VALLEY, SPARSELY POPULATED BY SCATTERED FARMSTEADS. ITS MOST NOTABLE FEATURE IS THE CHAIN OF THREE CONSIDERABLE RESERVOIRS, ALL MANAGED BY NORTHUMBRIA WATER, SUPPLYING THE NEEDS OF THE LARGE INDUSTRIAL/RESIDENTIAL AREAS A FEW MILES AWAY.

Built in 1894, Hury is the oldest, followed by Blackton (1896) and Balderhead (1965). The water authority has a visitor-friendly policy, which has led to the creation of car parks, picnic areas and nature reserves.

Most notable is Hannah's Meadow at Low Birk Hat Farm. In the 1980s a television documentary vividly depicted the struggles, particularly during severe winter weather, of Hannah Hauxwell, an elderly lady who operated the family farm, Low Birk Hat, in a completely traditional manner, without artificial fertilisers. The farm was without electricity or running water. One result of this relatively primitive farming was North Pennine hay meadows, rich in wild flowers. One of the meadows has been preserved as 'Hannah's Meadow', with a collection of a few of her farming implements in a barn at the adjacent High Birk Hat Farm.

The legendary Pennine Way long-distance footpath from Edale in Derbyshire to the Scottish border passes the end of Blackton Reservoir and along the edge of Hannah's Meadow.

THE BASICS

Distance: 2¼ miles / 3.5km

Gradient: Steady ascent from reservoir to road, approximately 170 feet (52m)

Severity: Moderate

Approx time to walk: 1¼ hrs

Stiles: None

Map: OS Explorer OL31, North Pennines

Path description: Excellent. Hard surfaces and good grass.

Start point: Car park/picnic area at edge of Balderhead Reservoir (GR NY 929188)

Parking: As start point, above, (DL12 9UX)

Dog friendly: On leads

Public toilets: At car park – may be locked

Nearest food: Two inns at Romaldkirk

1. Set off down the unsurfaced vehicular track passing in front of the public convenience building (which may be closed). The descent is steady, winding down the slope below the great dam of Balderhead Reservoir.

2. At the bottom go through a wide gate; to the right is Blackton Bridge and the head of the reservoir of the same name. Do not cross. Turn left along a waymarked inviting grass track, soon rising towards the buildings of Low Hat Farm, former home of Hannah Hauxwell. This is part of the Pennine Way. A board has information concerning Blackton Nature Reserve.

3. Go through a 'Pennine Way' gate, and then turn left at a signpost in 20 yards to follow the farm access drive, steadily uphill, with Hannah's Meadow on the left.

4. Well up the hill, turn left to walk along a boardwalk towards High Birk Hat Farm and the barn, with a few preserved relics of Hannah's occupation of the lower farm. Return to the drive, turning left to continue the ascent. Join the Baldersdale road, turning left to walk by the roadside to the gates which mark the turning to the car park/picnic area.

5. Turn left to walk by the roadside to the car park.

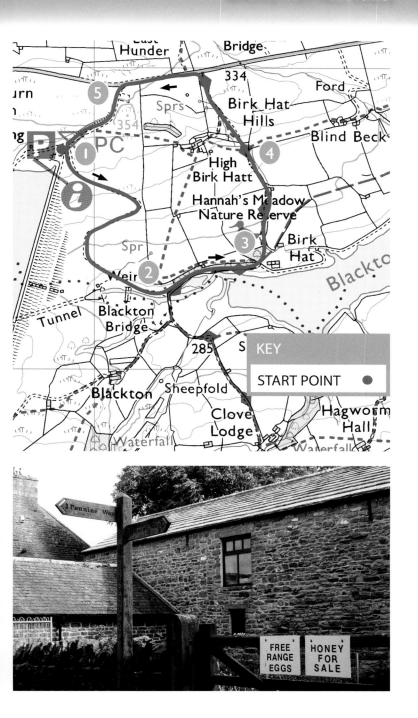

BOWES

A straightforward circuit linking Bowes village with the nearby countryside, twice crossing the charming River Greta and passing through agricultural countryside.

Having been bypassed by the busy A66 main road, Bowes is a quiet village, an unpretentious place with old stone houses and some interesting features. The Roman fort of Lavatrae was built to protect the road which ran over what is now known as the Stainmore Pass. Virtually all the stone from the fort was taken for re-use in more recent buildings such as the castle, the church and the churchyard.

Superimposed on the fort was Bowes Castle, at the time of King Henry II, about 1170. Of the castle, only the former keep remains, a solidly built ruin. The castle suffered so much from attacks by Scottish raiders that by the middle of the 14th century is was considered to be worthless. In its turn the castle has been robbed of much of its stone for the construction of houses in the village. The remains are in the care of English Heritage. The adjacent church of St Giles is the same age as the castle.

Charles Dickens stayed at the 16th century Unicorn, a coaching inn now known as the Ancient Unicorn in the main street at Bowes, while researching for Nicholas Nickleby (published in 1838). This was the place where schoolboys bound for the notorious Dotheboys Hall school left their coach. The inn is allegedly haunted by the ghost of the daughter of a former landlord, who lost the will to live following the unfortunate death of her lover.

Dotheboys Hall was based on an actual school, William Shaw's Academy, in Bowes. The proprietor, William Shaw, became the model for Dickens's evil head, Wackford Squeers. William Shaw and many of the school pupils are buried in the St Giles churchyard. Inside the church is a memorial to one former pupil.

It should be noted that the famous Bowes Museum is on the fringe of Barnard Castle, not at Bowes. It was built for John and Josephine Bowes, from whom it takes its name.

THE BASICS

Distance: 2¼ miles / 3.75km
Gradient: No steep hills, overall ascent only around 100 feet (30m)
Severity: An easy short walk
Approx time to walk: 1¼ hrs
Stiles: Six
Map: OS Explorer OL31, North Pennines
Path description: Some surfaced roadway, otherwise good footpaths
Start point: Car park opposite Village Institute, Bowes village (GR NY 996136)
Parking: Car park in Bowes as above (DL12 9HU)
Dog friendly: On leads
Public toilets: None on route
Nearest food: Inn on main street, Bowes village

BOWES WALK

1. Cross the road and walk along Back Lane, a quiet little road, rising gently towards Bowes Castle. The valley of the River Greta is below to the left.

2. At the castle turn left through a little gate with a 'Pennine Way' signpost, followed by a farm gate. Bear right to stay quite close to the fence along the top of a large meadow. Go over a stile and continue along much the same line, passing a waymark on a post. Go over another stile; there is now a wall on the left. Go over three more stiles before reaching a final stile giving access to a farm road.

3. Turn left to follow the road, soon going through a gate to pass a sizeable farm (Swinholme). After the farm, the track, now unsurfaced, bends to the right to descend to the river. Go ahead to pass a weir and cross the river on a footbridge.

4. After the bridge bear right, across a meadow to a wall with a farm gate and a 'Pennine Way' signpost. Turn left to join a farm roadway.

5. Turn left to walk along the roadway, passing West Pasture and West Gates farms before reaching Grimonby hamlet. At West Gates the roadway bears right to avoid going through the farm.

6. At Grimonby, turn left at a 'T' junction, cross Grimonby Bridge and rise gently back to the car park.

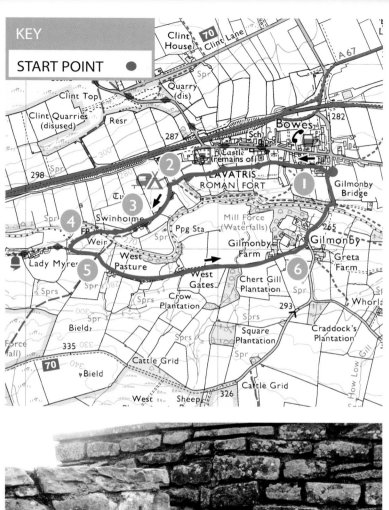

KEY

START POINT ●

COTHERSTONE

A CIRCULAR COUNTRY WALK BASED ON THE ATTRACTIVE AND SUBSTANTIAL VILLAGE OF COTHERSTONE, FOUR MILES (6.5KM) NORTH-WEST OF BARNARD CASTLE. FOR A COMPARATIVELY SHORT WALK, THE ROUTE HAS A SURPRISING VARIETY OF SCENERY — FARMING LAND, PARKLAND, WOODED RIVER VALLEY AND PART OF THE VILLAGE STREET.

The long village street at Cotherstone rises gently past the Fox and Hounds Inn, with a small green in front, a newsagent/general store, the village school and a variety of solid old stone-built houses, before reaching a small triangular green, on the left. The Green has a small stream, with a stone bridge. A road leading to the parish church and to Bowes goes to the right.

Nearby, the River Tees runs in a most attractive valley, beautifully wooded. This route links the village with the river valley.

A Quaker Meeting House stands lonely across a field, reached by an extension of the walk, described below.

THE BASICS

Distance: 2 miles / 3km (not including visit to Quaker Meeting House)

Gradient: No steep hills; one flight of steps

Severity: Easy, total ascent approximately 100 feet (30m)

Approx time to walk: 1 hr

Stiles: Two

Maps: OS Explorer OL31, North Pennines

Path description: Surfaced road in village, firm roadway to farm, good grass tracks along riverside, lane back to village

Start point: Roadside at junction of B6277 with Mire Lane (GR NY 013193)

Parking: Roadside as close to Mire Lane as possible (DL12 9PW)

Dog friendly: On leads across farming land

Public toilets: None

Nearest food: Fox and Hounds Inn, Cotherstone village

COTHERSTONE WALK

1. Start by leaving the village street along Mire Lane, a very minor roadway leading to Cooper House. There is no name on the roadway; it is found less than 50 yards south of the junction with the road to the church, on the opposite side of the village street. There is a 'public footpath' signpost. The lane has tarmac underfoot, with grass along the middle, lined with bluebells and ransoms in May, passing through farmland, basically level but with one fall and rise to cross a small stream. There is one waymarked gateway, with a 'private road' notice. Continue. As the buildings of Cooper House come into view, the farmland has much of the character of parkland.

2. Reach a gate at Cooper House and turn left, as indicated by a waymark, to follow the boundary past the farm buildings to a waymarked kissing gate. Follow the route indicated by waymarks – the Teesdale Way – to take a distinct path over grass gradually descending the river

bank. Pass a waymark on a post to reach a waymarked stile and a footbridge over a stream. Continue, now quite close to the river, to another waymarked stile and a flight of stone steps up the side of the valley. The path passes through woodland, across the foot of a long-disused quarry and over a stile, before rising to join a wider track.

3. Bear right at this junction (waymark) and stay with this excellent track back towards Cotherstone. The spire of the church is occasionally in view to the left.

4. Reach the fringe of the village, turning left at the village street to walk past The Green, with its stream and bridge and return to the parking place. Note – a left turn at the bottom end of The Green leads to a lane and then a signposted footpath along the edge of a field to reach the isolated Quaker Friends Meeting House (notice board at The Green). To access the Fox and Hounds Inn or the shop turn right on joining the village street.

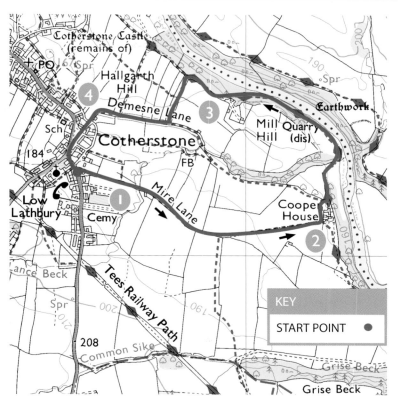

AN EXCELLENT CIRCUIT CONNECTING TOWN WITH ABBEY, WITH MANY INTERESTING FEATURES EN ROUTE.

With the ruin of its once great castle and its long, climbing, main street, lined with handsome old buildings, Barnard Castle is a delightful small town, bustling with activity, particularly on market days. The River Tees fringes the town, below the castle, with excellent footpaths on both sides. The castle was founded in the late 11th century. The town received its market charter in 1178; the market cross is a very dominant and distinctive octagonal structure. Also important is Blagraves House of the early 16th century. The King's Head Hotel hosted Charles Dickens in 1838, while he was writing Nicholas Nickleby. Barnard Castle was noted for its array of water-powered mills; the remains of one mill are passed on this walk.

Egglestone Abbey sits serenely on a knoll above the south bank of the river. The abbey was founded by the Premonstratensian order in 1195 and closed in 1540. The substantial remains, vandalised over the centuries for stone used to construct nearby buildings, are in the care of English Heritage; there is no charge for admission.

Once a toll bridge, Abbey Bridge of 1773 spans a deep limestone gorge close to the abbey, its lofty arch being 62 feet (19m) high.

On the fringe of Barnard Castle and visible from this walk is the French chateau-like building housing the remarkable collection of the Bowes Museum, claimed by some to be one of the most interesting museums in the country and well worth a visit.

THE BASICS

Distance: 2¾ miles / 4.5km

Gradient: No steep hills

Severity: Generally easy walking

Approx time to walk: 1½ hours

Stiles: Three

Map: OS Explorer OL31, North Pennines

Path description: Good footpaths, minor road, farm roadway

Start point: Demesnes recreation area, Barnard Castle (GR NZ 051161)

Parking: Informal recreation area (Demesnes) at the outward end of Gray Lane (off Thorngate), adjacent to children's play area. Two-metre high overhead entrance barrier (DL12 8PB)

Dog friendly: On leads

Public toilets: In Barnard Castle

Nearest food: Wide choice in Barnard Castle

BARNARD CASTLE WALK

1. Set off along the inviting track across the grassy area, with the river to the right. Go through a gate, keeping right to reach the site of a former mill, with cottages and with a great weir to the right. Continue along the path which, although rather faint over grass in places, is never in doubt. At a gate with two waymarks, keep right, as close to the river as possible.

2. Keep right to pass between the boundary of a sewage works and the river. After passing the works note the rock scarp above to the left.

3. Rise steadily to a gate to join a road, turning right to walk by the roadside to the magnificent Abbey Bridge. Cross the bridge, turning right to continue by the side of a quiet road as far as the entrance to the ruins of the abbey. Divert to the left to rise to the abbey.

4. Return to the valley road, turning left. Look out for a charming little bridge (former packhorse?) superseded by the more modern bridge alongside.

5. As the road bends left, rising, look out for a signposted footpath, through a squeezer stile, on the right. A clear path follows the edge of several fields, gently uphill and well above the river. There is another (easy) stile. The splendid chateau-like Bowes Museum is in view across the valley.

6. Bear to the right to descend and join a caravan site access roadway at another easy stile. Go right to follow the main road through the site. At the far end are two adjacent waymarks; keep right, downhill, then turn sharp left in 20 yards to leave the site on a narrow path which continues, close to the river as far as a footbridge.

7. Cross the bridge, leading to the bottom end of Thorngate. Rise along the roadside pavement. Turn right along Gray Lane to return to the car park.

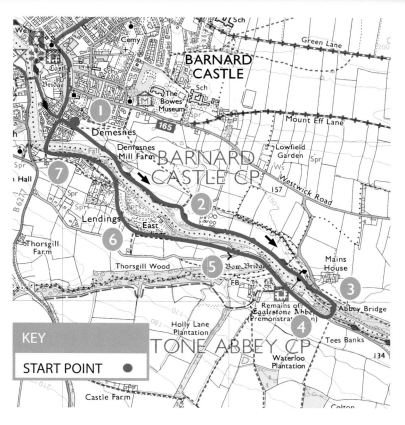

KEY

START POINT •

GAINFORD & PIERCEBRIDGE

A LINEAR WALK ALONG PART OF THE TEESDALE WAY, CONNECTING TWO FINE VILLAGES WITH A RETURN BY USING THE DARLINGTON TO BARNARD CASTLE BUS SERVICE.

Two of the most attractive villages in the lower part of Teesdale, Gainford and Piercebridge both have huge, well-maintained greens. Gainford has a village store and a butcher's shop.

Close to Gainford is a fountain yielding mineral-rich water. Discovered in the 18th century, this source soon achieved the status of a spa, attracting numerous visitors from the Darlington area and prompting the construction of guest houses around the Green. Its popularity faded by the start of World War I and the coping was damaged by vandals. In 2002 replacement fittings were provided.

Another feature of Gainford is the former Academy, fronting the Green. The late Arthur Stanley Jefferson, better known as Stan Laurel of Laurel and Hardy fame, spent three years as a boarder at the Academy, which closed in 1899. It has subsequently been converted to housing.

Located at an important crossing point of the River Tees, Piercebridge has the site of an important Roman fort, some of which is very accessible and well laid out for visitors. To carry their major highway, Dere Street, across the river, the Romans also built the first Pierce Bridge, a little way downstream of the present bridge.

THE BASICS

Distance: 2¼ miles / 4km

Gradient: Level walk

Severity: Easy walking

Number of stiles: One (avoidable)

Map: OS Explorer 304, Darlington and Richmond

Path description: Modest length of roadside pavement. Excellent grassy path alongside the River Tees

Start point: The Green at Gainford (GR NZ 170167)

Parking: Informal parking around The Green at Gainford (DL2 3DS)

Dog friendly: On leads

Public toilets: none

Nearest food: Inns at Gainford and Piercebridge, cafe/farm shop at Piercebridge, tea room at Gainford

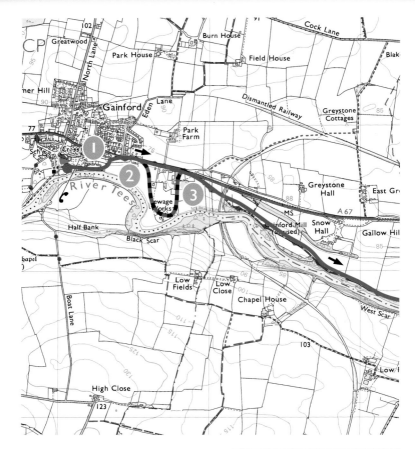

1. From a parking place anywhere on The Green, head east towards the narrow end, passing a coffee shop and the former Academy. Join the main road through the village by the front of the Lord Nelson Inn. Continue along the roadside pavement for almost 400 yards, passing the Gainford surgery and a huge brick building on the way.

2. (Note – This length of roadside can be avoided by turning right at a footpath sign immediately before the surgery and

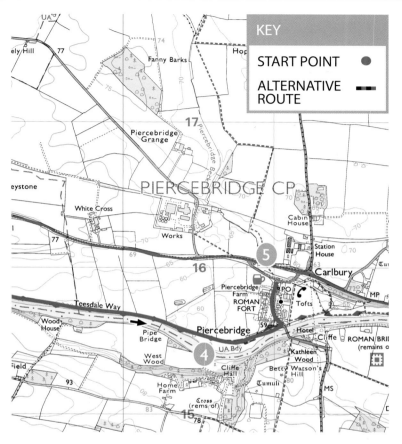

following a clear path which loops to the left, close to a very scenic section of the river before rising to join a sewage works access roadway leading to the road beside the brick building. This variation adds approximately a quarter-mile (0.5km) to the length of the walk.)

3.   Just after the end of the roadside pavement descend to a kissing gate on the right. Follow the 'Teesdale Way' sign, bearing left to follow a waymarked track between fences. Cross a little stream and go over a

stile, passing horse paddocks on the way to another stile. Cross a bridge to a waymarked stile. There is a huge hay meadow to the left as the path joins another track from the right, with the river now close on the right. There are waymarks on a post; go through a gate and continue. The way is never in doubt, keeping just above the steep river banking, well wooded and carpeted with bluebells and other wild flowers in May. Cross another little stream. Go through more waymarked gates before reaching a substantial house.

4. Go through a gate and bear right then left to pass the house, joining its surfaced drive. Follow the drive, rising gently to Piercebridge village. Go right to pass a row of garages before joining the public road, over a stile. To the right is the famous bridge, with the George Inn beyond. To the left is the village green, with a turning to the right to visit the signposted Roman fort and a turn to the left to the farm shop and tea room.

5. Continue beyond the top of the green to reach a main road. Twenty yards to the right of the junction is the bus stop with the half-hourly service back to Gainford (Lord Nelson Inn).

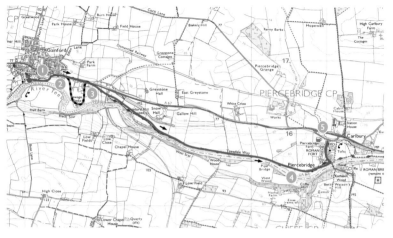

HAMSTERLEY FOREST

A GENTLE WALK WITHIN THE LARGEST FOREST IN COUNTY DURHAM.

The huge expanse of Hamsterley Forest (5,000 acres) includes more variety of landscape than would normally be expected in what is, essentially, a commercial enterprise. It is by no means all regimented coniferous trees; there are plenty of broad-leafed species and even hay meadows are included within this most attractive forest.

Public access is catered for to an exceptional degree; in addition to the comprehensive visitor centre there are several other car parks/picnic areas and a linking road (Forest Drive) running most of the length of the forest. There is a cycling centre with bicycle hire and there are recommended trails for cyclists. In addition to the cafe, the visitor centre has an information room.

One enterprising initiative is the 'Gruffalo Trail' for children, setting out a route with frequent sign boards and models which encourage the children to think about and to investigate features of the environment. The Bedburn Beck runs attractively through the forest.

THE BASICS

Distance: 1¾ miles / 3km

Gradient: No steep or prolonged hills, only one modest rise

Severity: Easy walking

Approx time to walk: 1 hr

Stiles: None

Map: OS Explorer OL31, North Pennines

Path description: Entirely good – tarmac and firm gravel. Some parts can be a little wet after rain.

Start point: Hamsterley Forest Visitor Centre (GR NZ 092312)

Parking: Hamsterley Forest Visitor Centre: pay and display (Nearest DL13 3NL)

Dog friendly: Yes, the forest is obviously popular with dog owners

Public toilets: Close to the visitor centre

Nearest food: Cafe is part of the visitor centre complex

1. Walking routes are well organised. From the visitor centre the 'Bedburn' area has three recommended routes, each colour coded and waymarked.

2. The 'blue, riverside' trail is the basic circuit described below; it can easily be extended to become the 'yellow' route or the 'orange' route.

3. Start at the bottom end of the car park, by the beck, turning right to pass between large stones. The first part of the track has been designed to facilitate use by pushchairs or wheelchairs. There are several signs confirming the route, including waymarks on a post. The track is level, close to the beck, soon passing a play area. At a cross paths go straight across, following the blue waymark. The path is narrower, possibly wet in places.

4. Join the Forest Drive road, bearing left to walk along the roadside pavement for a short distance. Fork left at a 'public footpath' signpost. Pass along the edge of a hay meadow, carpeted with cowslips in May, to reach a bridge over a tributary stream, followed by a picnic area, bearing right to rejoin Forest Drive.

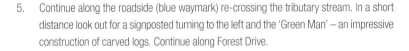

5. Continue along the roadside (blue waymark) re-crossing the tributary stream. In a short distance look out for a signposted turning to the left and the 'Green Man' – an impressive construction of carved logs. Continue along Forest Drive.

6. In a further 100 yards along the road go left at a fork, rising to leave Forest Drive on a surfaced road, passing in front of two detached houses. Go past a vehicular barrier and turn right at a junction in a few yards. Follow a pleasant woodland path to a junction with a similar path.

7. Turn right, downhill, soon re-joining Forest Drive; bear left to return to the visitor centre in 200 yards.

KEY

START POINT ●

West Hoppyland Allotments

West Ho

Mill Plantation

Low Redford Allotments

Hatcase

Low Redford Wood 148

Resr

ORIENTEERING

ORNAMENTAL DRIVE

Low Redford

Redf
Bridge

Bedburn Beck

Windy Bank

k Wood

Windy

B

SOUTH BEDBURN CP

ntation

08

09

BISHOP AUCKLAND

A CIRCUIT WHICH INCLUDES PART OF THE TRACKBED OF A DISUSED RAILWAY LINE (THE AUCKLAND WAY), PATHS ACROSS FARMING LAND, A LENGTH BESIDE THE RIVER WEAR, AND PART OF THE CENTRE OF BISHOP AUCKLAND. EFFECTIVELY IT CIRCUMNAVIGATES THE PARKLAND (800 ACRES OR SO) OF AUCKLAND CASTLE.

A good-sized market town situated twelve miles (19km) to the south-west of Durham, Bishop Auckland has a long history much conditioned by its status as the home of the formerly powerful Prince Bishops since 1190. The castle has undergone many transformations over the centuries, becoming the official residence of the Bishop as late as 1832. The last of the Prince Bishops died in 1836. The castle and its substantial park are now visitor attractions, with a tea room. Subject to winter restrictions they are open to the public.

There is a good shopping centre, whilst the area around the town hall, built in 1862, and by the entrance gates to the castle park has certain elegance.

Industrially, the town was at the heart of the great 19th-century Durham coal mining activity which lasted until the last deep mine closed in 1968. Coupled with this industry was the local proliferation of railways, mostly now closed, as evidenced by the Auckland Way, part of the route set out below. The town does still have a railway service.

Below the built-up area, the open space by the side of the River Wear is attractive, with a minor road leading to the Roman fort of Vinovia.

THE BASICS

Distance: 3½ miles / 5.5km

Gradient: One steep ascent in Bishop Auckland. Overall ascent almost 300 feet (90m)

Severity: Moderately demanding

Approx time to walk: 2 hours

Stiles: Nine

Map: OS Explorer 305, Bishop Auckland

Path description: Former railway line (well compacted) and riverside path

Start point: Small car park/picnic area at New Coundon, north-east of Bishop Auckland (GR NZ 229301)

Parking: As start point. Entrance to the car park is directly off the A688 (DL14 8QB)

Dog friendly: The Auckland Way is much used by dog walkers; there are disposal facilities. On leads only through the farming land and the town.

Public toilets: In Bishop Auckland

Nearest food: Wide choice in Bishop Auckland; inn at New Coundon

BISHOP AUCKLAND WALK

1. From the car park turn right, along the Auckland Way, a pleasant walking route, largely on an embankment, giving long views, initially over a golf course on the left. The track rises gently, soon crossing over a steep-sided valley. Reach two solidly built overbridges.

2. Turn right at the far side of the first bridge to rise up a flight of steps, bearing left at the top to walk to a stile. Go over and turn left to cross the bridge. Continue along the left edge of a huge meadow, close to a hedge, descending gently. The path is vague, over short grass. For most of this long descent there is the stone boundary wall of the Auckland Castle parkland. Go over a waymarked stile, still descending the side of the valley of the River Wear. Close to a corner of the wall there is a rough, stony and wet section of the path, with a little stream on the right. Go over two more stiles to continue the descent.

3. Go over another stile to join a public road. Cross over to a little path along the grassy bank above the River Wear, turning left towards the town and passing the confluence of the River Gaunless with the Wear at Jock's Bridge. Continue to a small pumping station. Turn left to re-join the road. Pass an information board and rise steeply up a town street to reach the Town Hall and its spacious Market Place.

4. Bear right then left past the Town Hall and St Anne's Chapel, then left towards the castle gates at 'Market Place'. Continue along the side of a main road towards Spennymoor, downhill.

5. Look carefully for a signposted public footpath on the left. Turn left to rise up a short flight of steps to a stile and a well-used path, possibly with some mud. Go over another stile and rise steadily along the edges of large cultivated fields, with the castle boundary wall on the left. Go over another stile to cross the golf club access road. The gradient eases; go over a stile to join the former railway line, turning right to return to the car park.

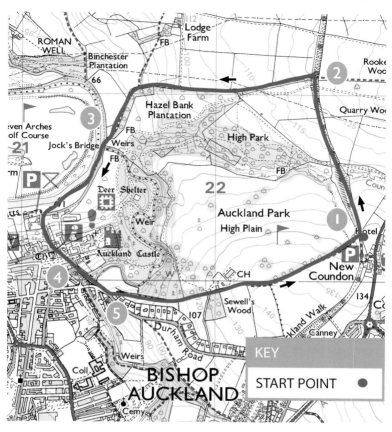

KEY

START POINT ●

ROMAN WELL

Lodge Farm

FB

Binchester Plantation

66

Rooke Woo

Hazel Bank Plantation

Quarry Woo

2

3

even Arches olf Course

High Park

21

Jock's Bridge

FB

Weirs

FB

Deer Shelter

Weir

22

Auckland Park

High Plain

FB

Hotel

P

New Coundon

134

Auckland Castle

CH

4

W

CH

Sewell's Wood

1

Durham Road

107

kland Walk

Canney

Co

5

Weirs

Coll.

BISHOP AUCKLAND

Cemy

SHINCLIFFE WOOD

A GENTLE WALK THROUGH THE LOWER PART OF THE ATTRACTIVE SHINCLIFFE WOOD WITH A RETURN PATH ABOVE THE BANK OF THE RIVER WEAR.

Despite its proximity to the city of Durham and to the former colliery village of High Shincliffe, Shincliffe is one of County Durham's 'green villages', a pleasant and peaceful place with church and green flanked by residential development. The centre of activity is the large garden centre, an emporium selling much more than plants, and with a comprehensive cafe, in the modern manner.

Covering much of the steep east side of the valley of the River Wear, Shincliffe Wood is an attractive mixture, rich in fauna and flora. Flowing below the woodland, the River Wear is at its most peaceful at Shincliffe.

Near the lower edge of the woodland, Shincliffe Hall is a late 18th-century structure, now used as accommodation by the University of Durham.

THE BASICS

Distance: 1¾ miles / 3km

Gradient: Basic walk is level. Suggested extension has steep ascent and descent.

Severity: Easy, but suggested extension is more demanding

Approx time to walk: 45 minutes

Stiles: None

Map: OS Explorer 308, Durham and Sunderland

Path description: Outward route good broad track, return more narrow

Start point: Poplar Tree Garden Centre in Shincliffe village (GR NZ 289406)

Parking: Parking is available at the start point, subject to being a customer at the garden centre or its coffee shop. There is a notice advising on the use of the large car park by walkers (DH1 2NG)

Dog friendly: Yes

Public toilets: None en route, see below

Nearest food: Brambles coffee shop, with toilets, at the garden centre

SHINCLIFFE WOOD WALK

1. Leave the garden centre by the vehicular access, turning sharp right to walk along the surfaced lane (Hall Lane).

2. In approximately a quarter of a mile (0.5km) there is a gate on the right. Ignore this, staying with the lane (Weardale Way) as it rises gently before descending towards the rear of Shincliffe Hall. Fork left, along a broad track, signposted to High Butterby Farm. This excellent track stays close to the bottom edge of Shincliffe Wood.

3. In approximately half a mile (1km), ten yards before reaching the bank of the river, turn right along a minor path raking back sharply. Although narrow and in places a little overgrown, this path is never in doubt as it stays above the river bank, with a hedge to the right. Pass through a little waymarked gate and below Shincliffe Hall, along a paved section of track. The path is now much wider as it returns to the gate at point 1. Retrace the outward route to the garden centre.

4. For a longer walk, with a steady ascent, continue along the Weardale Way at point 2. After the ascent of the valley side, the track continues past High Butterby Farm before a left turn is made in a little less than half a mile (under 1km), along Strawberry Lane, an ancient bridleway. In almost one mile (1.5km) turn left, leaving the lane, to head for West Grange Farm, followed by a descent through the woods to rejoin the outward route fairly close to the rear of Shincliffe Hall. Turn right to return to the garden centre car park.

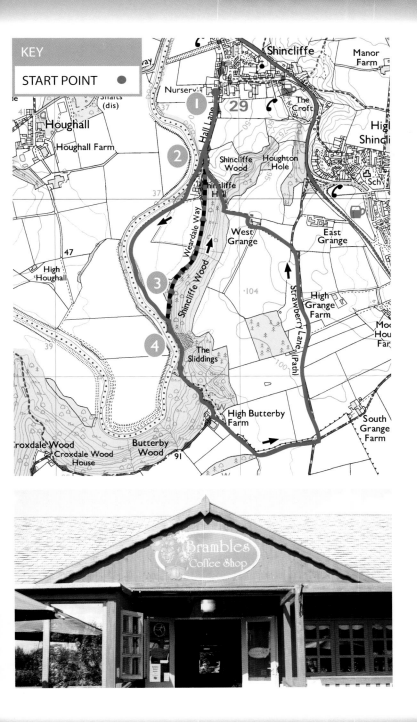

DURHAM CITY

A COMBINATION OF THE WONDERFUL AND HISTORIC CITY
CENTRE WITH A RIVERSIDE STROLL.

The fine and ancient city of Durham has a peninsula set high over a loop in the River Wear as its crown. On this peninsula the cathedral and the castle face each other across

the spacious Palace Green, accompanied by a Heritage Centre and Museum, a World Heritage Site Visitor Centre and the Assembly Rooms; truly a magnificent array of enormous historical significance.

After a leisurely stroll by the side of the river, with a sculpture and bandstand, the walking route set out below ascends to reach Palace Green as a great climax before returning to the starting point at Elvet Bridge.

THE BASICS

Distance: 2 miles / 3km

Gradient: Ascent to Palace Green is at a reasonable gradient

Severity: Generally easy

Approx time to walk: 1 hour

Stiles: None

Map: OS Explorer 308, Durham and Sunderland

Path description: Almost all on hard-surfaced tracks and roadways

Start point: At the higher (city) end of Elvet Bridge (GR NZ 275425)

Parking: No particular car park is recommended. There is plenty of street parking beyond the bridge, along Old Elvet and its side roads (near DH1 3AQ)

Dog friendly: On leads by the river bank; less friendly in the city centre

Public toilets: Palace Green.

Nearest food: Inns and cafes en route, Cafe on the Green at Palace Green

DURHAM CITY WALK

1. From the start point at the higher end of Elvet Bridge, go left to descend a long flight of steps. There is a sign at the top for boating and the river. Pass the Boathouse Inn and continue along a track by the side of the river, as far as a little footbridge.

2. Turn right to cross the bridge and then left to continue along a surfaced track with the river now on the left and playing fields to the right. Pass a modern sculpture of a cow and a bandstand.

3. Pass the premises of a rowing club, bending to the right to stay with the same track, now rising gently, with a minor road to the left. Pass Durham City Cricket Club. At a junction go left, uphill, to join a road. Pass across the top of a leafy little square to go past massive stone pillars, pass the County Court and head for the cathedral. Pass the Court Inn, with the police station to the right,

4. Turn left at a main road (New Elvet). Pass the Students' Union. In 200 yards turn right, up a few shallow steps, signposted to the cathedral. Cross high over the river on Kingsgate Bridge, again signposted to the cathedral (and the Heritage Centre). Continue over the cobbles of Bow Lane, turn right, pass the entrance to the museum and heritage centre, then turn left in 20 yards, along Dun Cow Lane, to pass the cathedral and reach Palace Green, a beautiful large open space, very much the heart of old Durham, with historic buildings around and the castle ahead.

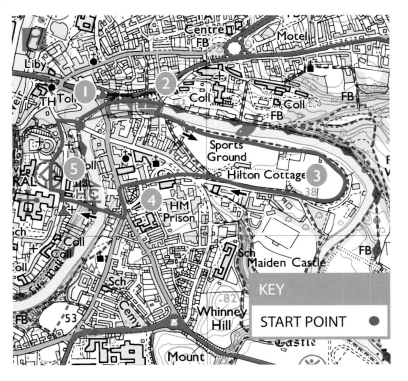

5. Pass the Cafe on the Green and leave the Green by Owengate, on the right, downhill. Pass the World Heritage Site Visitor Centre. At a junction keep left, along Saddler Street. Opposite the second Waterstones shop turn sharp right, down a few steps to head for Elvet Bridge and the start point of the walk.

iStock

iStock

SEAHAM

Until a few years ago the Durham coast was one of Britain's great coal producing areas. There were numerous pits and vast quantities of spoil were dumped along the coastline.

A huge clearing operation has been of great local benefit, leading to the creation of the Durham Coast Path and several nature reserves in this much-improved area.

The Londonderry family of Seaham Hall were the great land and colliery owners of the Seaham area. Seaham harbour was developed in the 19th century, with a railway line to transport coal from the inland pits to ships in the harbour.

The church of St Mary the Virgin, in what used to be the village of Old Seaham, is one of very few Anglo-Saxon structures which pre-date the arrival of the Viking invaders.

THE BASICS

Distance: 3 miles / 4.75km

Gradient: Short steep rise from promenade to car park, otherwise almost level

Severity: An easy walk

Approx time to walk: 1½ hrs

Stiles: None

Map: OS Explorer 308, Durham and Sunderland

Path description: Hard-surfaced tracks, roadways and promenade

Start point: Large car park, picnic area, cafe and public conveniences at Seaham Hall Beach at the northern edge of Seaham (GR NZ 422508)

Parking: Seaham Hall Beach car park, as above (SR7 7AD)

Dog friendly: On leads, with particular care through the town. Beach adjacent on return part of walk.

Public toilets: At car park and inside Byron shopping centre

Nearest food: Cafe at car park; many inns and cafes in Seaham town

1. From the car park walk towards the sea. By the steps at the top of a way down to the beach, turn right at a 'Durham Coast Path' fingerpost. Join the road at another fingerpost, turning left along the pavement. Across the road is a boundary wall of the Seaham Hall Estate.

2. At the end of the wall, in approximately 150 yards, cross the road to walk along Church Lane, leading to the Anglo-Saxon Church of St Mary the Virgin. At the church go past a barrier to a footpath, bearing round to the left. Seaham Hall is soon in view to the right and the excellent path crosses a wide, rather overgrown bridge. In approximately 35 yards there is a tiny path on the right with a flight of narrow and muddy steps leading down to an old ice house. Continue along the main path, going to the left at a junction. This broad track is known as the New Drive, built for Lady Londonderry after her husband's death in 1864 to facilitate travel between the Hall and her offices at the harbour.

3. There is a fence on the left and playing fields to the right. Pass the end of a modern cycleway and continue, the track still unsurfaced. Reach a surfaced road, passing Seaham Harbour Cricket Club, on the right. Go straight ahead through residential development, soon reaching Seaham railway station, on the right.

4. Follow the road as it bends to the left; turn right, past barriers to join a wide trackway, a former railway line heading towards the harbour. Turn left to descend gently along this broad track. To the left are a road and the Roman Catholic Church of St Mary Magdalene. Pass under several bridges before reaching the end of the walkway, close to Seaham shopping centre.

5. Turn right, along Adelaide Row. Turn left at Church Street, the pedestrianised heart of Seaham town. At the bottom of the street, the modern Byron Shopping Centre, with public conveniences, is to the right. Turn left; in approximately 100 yards is a sculpture, The Brothers – waitin' t' gan down by Brian Brown. Continue by crossing the road near Barclays Bank and diverting to the right to view the historic harbour. Return to the road, turning right to continue along North Terrace, with its array of catering establishments and a statute of the sixth Marquess of Londonderry.

KEY

START POINT ●

6. Turn right, down a few steps, at an 'E.C.P.' Fingerpost to join a footpath which stays parallel with the road. There is also a waymark on a post and a memorial to local lifeboatmen who perished at sea. Go down a long flight of steps to join a lower, wider, promenade. Continue in the same direction, with views of Sunderland ahead. Those wishing to avoid the steps can go a little further, along the road, before descending a ramp to reach the lower promenade.

7. On reaching the sandy Seaton Hall Beach and the end of the promenade, turn left to ascend a long flight of steps and reach the road, just 30 yards from the car park/picnic area.

ABOUT THE AUTHOR

Following a professional career, when he retired in 1988, Norman Buckley and his wife June commenced writing guide books; these have mainly been walking guides but have included visitor guides.

Almost forty books have so far been published, covering areas in the United Kingdom and Western Europe. A speciality has been the popular 'Level Walks' series. Over much of the same period, Norman and June have worked as walking consultants for a major holiday organisation.

Revelevant interests include photography, travel, railways and industrial archaeology Norman holds a Diploma in Environmental Management (Liverpool University) and a Master of Arts Degree in Lake District Studies (Lancaster University). The author is a member of the Guild of Outdoor Writers and Photographers.

Norman and June have lived in the Lake District since 1990.